The TREE HOUSE

written by Jeremy Strong
illustrated by Jim Kavanagh

Chapter One

Cleo Puts on a Performance

Donut was watching a football match on television. His favourite team was winning. Donut sat at one end of the sofa and bounced up and down. Cleo sat at the other end of the sofa. Her arms were folded crossly over her chest.

Suddenly Donut's team scored a goal. "Yeah! Hurrah!" he yelled, and he bounced even harder. He bounced so hard that Cleo was catapulted off the other end of the sofa.

She landed in a heap on the floor. “Ow! That hurt!”

“Sorry,” said Donut. Cleo scowled at her big brother. She picked up the remote control and switched channels on the TV. Suddenly the TV had gone from football to ‘Jungle Vet.’ A monkey was having its tail bandaged.

“Put it back on the football!” yelled Donut. He tried to snatch the remote control from Cleo.

“No,” she snapped. “I’m watching a poor monkey with a bent tail.”

“I was watching the football before you!” bellowed Donut. Icarus the parrot flapped his wings. “Give me remote! Give me remote!” he squawked.

Donut made another grab for the remote control and twisted it from Cleo’s hand. Cleo wasn’t hurt, but she burst into tears anyway. Cleo was good at doing anything dramatic. Bursting into tears was one of Cleo’s best performances. She sat on the floor and sobbed, and sobbed and sobbed. Donut rolled his eyes in despair. He could see where all this was going to lead.

Sure enough, Mrs Pringle hurried into the room. She swept Cleo into her arms, "My little bubby baby, are you all right?"

Cleo gave her mother a look full of hopeless despair. "I was watching a poorly monkey and Donut snatched the remote and put it on the football. He hurt my hand." Cleo's lower lip trembled.

Cassandra Pringle turned to Donut. "Give me that remote," she ordered.

"But ..."

"No 'buts.' Give me the remote." Mrs Pringle switched the TV back onto 'Jungle Vet.' Now the vet was giving cough medicine to a sick lion.

Cleo sat down on the sofa. She smirked at her brother.

Donut leaped up, hurled himself out of the room in a fury and went stamping upstairs to his room. On the landing, Mr Pringle was struggling into his work overalls. “You look brassed off,” he said. Donut told his stepfather what had happened. Mr Pringle rolled his eyes. “Sisters, eh? What can you do?”

“Did you have a sister when you were my age?” Donut asked Colin.

“No, I had two aunts, and that was far worse.”

“Nothing can be worse than a little sister,” Donut muttered darkly.

“Well, you try out this nightmare for size. I had two aunts. They used to stink of the most dreadful perfume. They both used bright red lipstick. Whenever they came to visit they would sweep me up in their arms and plant kisses all over my face. It was like being slobbered to death by octopuses. My face ended up covered with big red lip marks. It was so embarrassing!”

Donut laughed.

Maybe Colin was right. Maybe two aunts *were* worse than one small sister.

"You'd better come with me," suggested Colin. "You can give me a hand with the garage I'm building on the side of the house."

Donut found some old clothes, and Colin handed him a hard hat.

"Always wear a helmet on a building site," said Colin. "There, you look like a real builder now!"

They went out to the garage. There were piles of earth lying around, where Colin had dug trenches for the foundations. There was a dirty orange concrete mixer standing amongst bags of sand and cement. Colin had put a big sheet of old wood on the ground to use as a mixing area. Old, dried up cement was stuck to it. It looked like a lunar landscape.

There was a mini JCB parked behind the garage. Colin had used it to dig the trenches. A big pile of new wooden beams lay nearby, ready to be used for the roof and the frames for the windows and doors. The garage walls were already in place, still surrounded by scaffolding. The concrete floor had just been laid.

"Make sure you don't walk on it," said Colin. "The bit at the back is hard and dry, but the front half only went down last night. It's still wet."

"What are we going to do?" asked Donut. Everything looked in such a mess. He couldn't think what they should do first.

"I'm going to start work on the roof," said Colin. "It will give the floor more time to dry off. You can help cut the roof beams to the right size and hand them up to me."

And that was exactly what they did. Donut went backwards and forwards, carrying great lengths of timber for his stepfather. Colin put on his goggles and dust mask. He marked the wood with the right measurements. He switched on his circular saw and got to work. The electric saw made short work of cutting through the wood.

"Brilliant!" said Colin. "Now we can put the roof on and it will really start looking like a garage. What sort of car do you think we should put inside? How about a Ferrari? I really fancy a big, red Ferrari. **VROOOM!** "

"I'd like a tank," growled Donut. He was still thinking about Cleo.

Chapter Two

Kitchen Catastrophe

Back inside the house Cleo sat on the sofa. She had switched off the TV because she didn't really want to watch it at all. Now she was bored. She sat on the sofa and sighed.

She could hear Colin and her big brother outside, talking and laughing. They were enjoying themselves, but she was bored.

Cleo wandered into the kitchen.
She looked in the fridge. She looked in the cupboards.
Maybe she could cook something.

A smile suddenly lit up Cleo's face. She had an idea, and it was a brilliant idea! She would make lunch for everyone. It would be a huge surprise and everyone would tell her how clever she was. They would eat the food and say that she was a wonderful cook.

Cleo began to daydream. She could imagine it all. She would be on TV – 'Cleo, the Kid who Cooks!' She would have her own TV series. She would be famous. People would ask her for her autograph. She would be rich!

Cleo took a quick stroll around the house to see what everyone was doing. Colin and Donut were outside. Her mother was doing some decorating in the bathroom. Good, that would keep all of them busy while she got on with lunch.

First of all Cleo needed the right equipment. She found an apron. It was a bit long, but it was a proper chef's apron so Cleo had to wear it. She couldn't find a real chef's hat so she had to use Colin's white baseball cap. That was a bit big too. It kept slipping down over her eyes.

Cleo got out a loaf of sliced bread. She was going to make sandwiches. She spread butter onto several slices

of bread. Then she began to look for something she could put in the sandwiches. Cleo found some lettuce, some yoghurt and some cheese. She got marmalade, peanut butter and chocolate spread. She found the salt and pepper, a tin of sardines, some cold meat, mayonnaise, apple sauce and mustard.

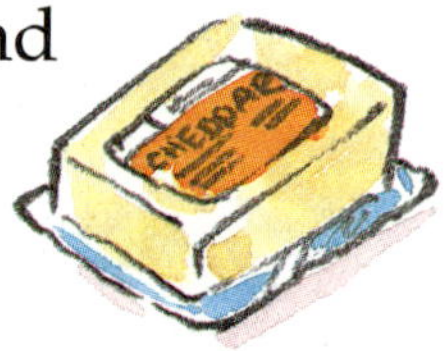

"My sandwiches are going to be brilliant!" Cleo said to herself cheerfully. She had often watched chefs on television. They always seemed to make such fantastic and unusual dishes. She thought that it was easy. "All I have to do is put unusual things together."

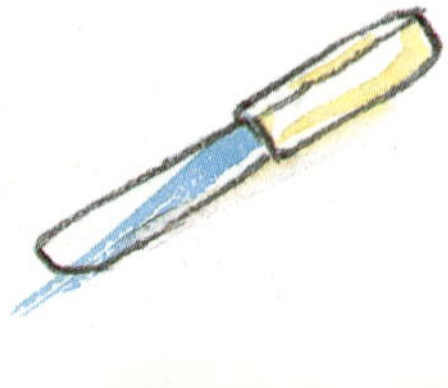

Cleo got to work. Lids came off jars. Spoons were dipped inside. Tins had their lids pulled off. Yoghurt and mayonnaise were dolloped onto slices of bread.

Cleo piled up her sandwiches one by one, until she had four big sandwich mountains.

Cleo went into the back room and laid the table. Then she looked at the clock. It was eleven o'clock. Oh well, lunch would have to be early today. She went into the hallway and yelled at the top of her voice. "Lunchtime everybody! Come and get it!"

Mrs Pringle called down from the top of the stairs. "Lunchtime? It's only eleven o'clock!"

Cleo stamped her foot. "Eat it before it goes cold," she ordered.

Donut put his head round the front door. When he saw Cleo in her huge apron and giant hat he burst out laughing.

"Don't laugh at me, or you won't get any lunch, and it's special lunch," snapped Cleo.

"But it's only eleven o'clock," Donut pointed out.

"I'm waiting," Cleo hissed. "Are you and Colin coming for lunch or not?"

Donut sighed. He knew there would be trouble if he and Colin didn't turn up, so he went and fetched him.

"Wash your hands," said Cleo.

Colin looked at Donut. They both looked at Mrs Pringle.

"Come on, boys. Wash your hands," said Mum.

"Now you can go and sit down," said Cleo. She waved the others into the back room and waited to see their looks of surprise and wonder and admiration.

Mum, Colin and Donut stared at the table. It was piled high with some very strange-looking sandwiches.

"Go on," said Cleo, pushing the cap away from her nose for the fiftieth time that morning. "Eat up."

"What's in them?" asked Colin warily as he picked up a sandwich.

"That one's chocolate spread, with sardines and a marmalade topping."

"Yes," said Colin, chewing very slowly. "It does taste just like that." His face had gone a greenish colour.

Cleo turned to her brother. "And the one you are eating has a special filling of yoghurt, mustard and grapes."

Donut suddenly rushed from the room with his hand over his mouth.

Mrs Pringle looked at her daughter. "Where did you get the recipes from?"

"My head," Cleo said proudly.

"Have you tried any of them yourself?"

"Not yet," said Cleo.

Mrs Pringle held out a sandwich. "Try this one," she suggested.

Cleo took a big bite. "Yum, yum," she said.

"Try chewing it," Colin said quietly.

Cleo began to chew. "Yum," she said with a smile. Then, "Oh! Ah! Hmmm. Urrr. Eeee. Ooooh!" And finally, "Yuk!"

Cleo shoved a hand over her mouth and went racing off in the same direction as her big brother. Donut watched with a grim smile as she stood over the toilet bowl and spat out the remains of her sandwich.

"I always thought that Mum was the worst cook in the world, but you, Cleo, you're a kitchen catastrophe!"

Chapter Three

Donut Walks the Plank

Colin and Donut worked on the garage for most of the afternoon. Donut had his eye on a pile of old wood that his stepfather had collected inside the garage. It was stacked on the bit of finished flooring at the back of the garage. There were several old planks and some thick pieces of strong timber.

"When we've finished I shall have to burn all that lot," Colin told Donut. "It's useless."

Donut couldn't take his eyes off the pile of wood. He thought about it all afternoon. In the end, Colin ran out of timber for the roof. He had to go off in his van to collect some from the timber yard. Donut stood at the open entrance to the garage. He just knew he could make something with the pile of wood. He was going to make something. He was going to make his own house, where anyone called Cleo was banned. All he had to do was get to the back of the garage without walking on the wet concrete.

Donut found a long plank. He put it on the ground and slowly pushed it out across the concrete. At last it reached the hard floor. Donut stood on the bridge he had made. He felt like a pirate, about to walk the plank.

Bit by bit he moved out across the floor until he reached the hard concrete. Donut let out a big sigh of relief. He gathered up a pile of timber and set off, back across the plank bridge. It wobbled, but he made it back safely.

Donut had soon made three journeys, gathering more and more wood. It was on the fourth journey that he ran into problems. Donut had his arms full with the last bits of wood from the pile. The plank began to wobble.

Donut struggled to keep his balance. The plank wobbled even more.

Donut knew he was going to fall. He shut his eyes.
The wood flew out of his arms as he tumbled backwards.

He lay on his back, arms and legs spread like a marooned starfish. Slowly, he sat up. He could feel great dollops of concrete sticking to his back and his hair.

Donut staggered to
his feet and looked down.
There was a perfect shape of his body left in the wet concrete. All around it lay bits of wood, like strange ships stuck in a frozen sea.

"Oh dear," Donut said quietly. He pulled the bits of wood from the concrete and carried them through to the back garden. This was where he had decided to build his house. It was not going to be on the grass. It was going to be up a tree. Donut wanted to be Tarzan, King of the Jungle, or at least Donut, King of Story Street.

He filled his pockets with big nails from Colin's tool box. He grabbed his stepfather's hammer, and he climbed the tree, pulling up the first piece of wood. Donut nailed it into place. Then he climbed down and got the second piece of wood.

By the time his stepfather came back from the timber yard Donut had almost finished the floor of his house. It was a rather bumpy floor, but Donut was pretty pleased. However, Colin was not pleased at all. "Donut!"

Donut peeped through the leaves of the tree. He bit his lip. Oh dear. Colin had noticed the garage floor.

"Donut!" Colin stormed into the back garden, still shouting. He stood right under the tree. Up above, Donut held his breath and tried not to move. He knew he was in big trouble.

Then the floor of his tree house gave way and Donut suddenly came crashing out of the tree. He landed on Colin's head and they both fell to the ground.

Neither of them were hurt, but the accident certainly hadn't improved Colin's temper. Donut thought Colin would never stop going on, but he did, at last. He sent Donut back into the house to have a bath and get the concrete out of his hair.

Cleo thought he was the funniest thing she had ever seen. Donut was really pleased when bedtime came at last and he could go to sleep. He had just had one of the worst days of his life.

Chapter Four

The Tree House

Donut was woken early next morning by the noise of the churning cement mixer. He rolled out of bed and went across to the window. Colin was already outside, working on the new garage. He was laying the concrete floor again. Donut decided that he had better keep well clear. Anyhow, he had work of his own to do on his tree house.

Cleo wandered into his bedroom and flopped into a chair. "What are you doing today?" she asked.

"I'm busy."

"Busy doing what?" Cleo went on.

"Busy avoiding you."

Cleo watched him as he pulled some clothes from the wardrobe. So, he was in one of those moods, was he? Cleo got up and padded back to her own room. She began to make plans of her own.

Once he was dressed and had eaten breakfast, Donut went out to the back garden. He gazed up the tree at the broken flooring. This time he would make it much better. This time it would be easy. This time it was going to be brilliant!

He climbed up into the tree. The first thing he did was nail back into place the floor planks that had fallen out. He must have used about thirty nails to each plank. Most of them bent as he hammered them in. Donut grew hotter and hotter, and crosser and crosser. The more cross he got, the more nails he bent.

The next thing to do was to build the walls. Donut stared down at the planks lying on the grass below. He stared at the tree branches around him. He stared into space and thought. He scratched his head. Building a tree house was not as easy as he had thought it would be. This was going to be difficult – very difficult.

At that moment there was a loud creak from under his feet and the end of one plank sprang away from its branch and shot up into the air, almost bashing Donut on the nose. Donut clenched his teeth. That was it! He'd had enough. He opened his mouth and roared with fury. "Aaaargh!" Then Donut sat down on the broken floor, with his head in his hands and sulked.

"Are you all right up there?" Colin was down below, gazing up into the branches.

"No. I'm not."

"I see you're making a tree house," Colin noted.

"I *was* making a tree house," growled Donut. "But now I'm making a tree mess."

"Bit difficult, eh?"

"The floor keeps breaking up," said Donut.

"Oh," Colin said, and he wandered away.

A minute later he came back, with a ladder. He put the ladder against the tree and climbed up to take a look at Donut's tree house.

"What you need is a couple of planks under the floor," Colin said, "Then you can lay the floor on top. You fix that end there, and I'll do this end."

Together they put in three joists for the floor. Then they nailed the floor planks onto the joists, instead of onto the branches. The floor was flatter and the nails didn't come out any more.

By this time Colin was working flat out. Donut spent most of the next two hours rushing up and down the ladder with different tools that his stepfather needed.

The three walls went up. Colin fixed a sloping roof on top.

The tree house was finished. Donut climbed inside and sat there with his stepfather, their legs dangling over the edge.

Cleo came out.

"Come on up!" yelled Donut. "It's brilliant."

Now three of them sat up there, in the high sunshine, with the dappled green leaves rustling around them.

"This tree house is fantastic," murmured Cleo. "I shall be Queen of the Trees and this will be my palace."

Donut's heart gave a lurch and stopped beating. Oh no. Cleo was at it again. He wanted to shout at her, but Colin was right next to him. Donut bit his lip and kept quiet.

"Well," Colin said slowly. "The thing is, Cleo, that this is Donut's tree house. I'm sure he won't mind you coming up here sometimes, but you will have to ask him first. This was his idea, and the tree house belongs to him."

Donut's heart began beating again. He smiled at his sister. "You can come up here anytime," he said.

"Good," said Cleo.

"Say 'Thank you, dearest brother,' Cleo," said Colin, laughing.

"Thank you, dearest brother."

"Remember that if Donut wants to be up here by himself, then that is up to him."

Cleo nodded.

Colin smiled again. "I'm hungry after all that work," he said. "How about some sandwiches?"

"I'll make them!" cried Cleo. "I've got some new ideas!"

"No! No!" shouted Donut. But Cleo was already down on the grass and racing for the kitchen.

Colin put an arm round Donut's shoulder. "I guess we shall be safer if we just stay here," he said. Donut grinned and nodded.

But there was no escape. Cleo did not wait for them to come to the kitchen. She took her special sandwiches out to the tree house instead. Mrs Pringle was with her.

"We made these together," said Mrs Pringle. "So they should be fine." Donut and Colin looked at each other. There was no escape. "Yum, yum," they said, bravely. Donut quietly got rid of most of his sandwich by dropping it out of the tree when nobody was looking.

Down below Fatcat was having a feast. She didn't seem to mind eating ham and jam sandwiches at all.